Healing Church Strife
in the
New Testament *and* Today

Healing Church Strife
in the
New Testament *and* Today

— Beyond Matthew 18:15–17 —

JAMES CHRISTENSEN
and THOMAS F. JOHNSON

WIPF & STOCK · Eugene, Oregon

HEALING CHURCH STRIFE IN THE NEW TESTAMENT
AND TODAY
Beyond Matthew 18:15–17

Wipf & Stock
An Imprint of Wipf and Stock Publishers
199 W. 8th Ave., Suite 3
Eugene, OR 97401

www.wipfandstock.com

PAPERBACK ISBN 13: 978-1-4982-3394-1
HARDBACK ISBN 13: 978-1-4982-3396-5

Manufactured in the U.S.A.   01/22/2016

But you, beloved, must remember the predictions of the apostles of our Lord Jesus Christ ... for they said to you, "In the last time there will be scoffers, indulging their own ungodly lusts." It is these worldly people, devoid of the Spirit, who are causing divisions. But you, beloved, build yourselves up on your most holy faith; pray in the Holy Spirit; keep yourselves in the love of God; look forward to the mercy of our Lord Jesus Christ that leads to eternal life. And have mercy on some who are wavering; save others by snatching them out of the fire; and have mercy on still others with fear, hating even the tunic defiled by their bodies.

JUDE 17–23

Contents

Preface

Not long ago I hired a contractor to build a new deck. I sketched out what I had in mind, particularly a deck low to the ground so there would be no need for a railing. He took one look at my work and commented, "You can draw anything, but that doesn't mean you can build it."

Much has been written about how to deal with strife in today's churches. There are many models and programs for doing so, and it is not our intention to add to that body of literature. There is also significant resistance to academic and professional ideas in this arena. That resistance takes shape as a retreat to simple principles, such as "love one another," "forgive one another," or as an appeal to apparently sufficient instructions such as Matthew 18:15–17. Both of these responses appeal to the New Testament, and that is what interests us enough to write this book. Having a quick sketch drawn from Scripture about what to do with church conflict is not the same as having a workable plan.

We began this project with a question: "Did New Testament churches actually do what is prescribed in Matthew 18:15–17 and similar texts?" We quickly discovered that they did not. This made us wonder, "What did New Testament era churches do about strife?" *The primary purpose of this book is to answer that question.* As we began to examine the New Testament from Matthew to Revelation, the great volume of conflict related information we found surprised us. Clearly, the common, simple appeals to Scripture had not gone far enough or deep enough. *So, a second purpose of this book is to shed light on that information.*

We identified and documented several strategies that New Testament churches used in dealing with conflict and with church "trouble-makers." Their use in that ancient historical and cultural context does not mean, however, that they can be easily and effectively used in our contemporary context. So, the practical value of New Testament experiences with church conflict for our time needs further exploration. And that constitutes *a third purpose of this book.*

Have we covered this topic completely? Far from it! Thus, *a fourth purpose of the book* is to invite further inquiry and dialogue about what the New Testament actually describes and teaches about church strife.

Introduction

Representatives from two opposing groups were gathered in a church that was about to be split. A long period of preparation had preceded this meeting, and a careful process leading toward possible reconciliation was underway. Issues were identified, feelings were being shared and explored, and apologies were being offered and accepted. Hopes for a good outcome were rising. Then, out of the blue, someone brought up Matthew 18:15–17, proclaiming that this was *the biblical model* that should be followed. That statement in that moment had the potential to derail a train that had already departed. The group was already moving forward by following an entirely different process. The appeal to Matthew 18:15–17 not only clashed with the immediate context, it also ignored the great weight of New Testament teaching about church conflict and how it might be treated. In studying what the Bible teaches about church strife, we use the terms, "New Testament churches," "the early Christian communities," and "followers of Jesus," as inclusive phrases for the various forms of groups (most often *ekklésiae*) and organizational structures portrayed in the New Testament, from the first disciples to fully developed churches with officers and procedures. We use the term "strife" to make a distinction between mere differences of opinion, which might be called conflicts, and stronger, more difficult, or more potentially destructive disputes.

Not every New Testament reference carries the same weight. Some disputes and their resolution changed the course of history, while others were more personal spats. While we have considered every reference that reflects strife within early Christian communities, we give the greatest attention to those cases that determined the nature of Christian faith and practice as we know it today.

Every book in the New Testament speaks directly to conflict within Christian communities or alludes to it. The theme appears in the Gospels' descriptions of conflict among the twelve apostles, particularly their concern over who is the greatest among them. Major portions of some of Paul's letters are directed toward conflict resolution, particularly Romans, 1 and 2 Corinthians, Galatians, and Ephesians.[1] Nevertheless, it appears that little attention is paid to this topic among New Testament students. For the most part those who give attention to church conflict either oversimplify the biblical material or pass over it lightly in favor of current techniques of conflict management. There is an unfortunate tendency among some who have not carefully looked into the New Testament to minimize the topic. For example, there is frequent reference to Matthew 18:15–17 as if it were the single answer when it comes to dealing with congregational conflict. On the other hand, an equally simple answer is sought in a vague appeal to "the rule of love." Some of the conflicts reflected in the New Testament involve two individuals; they are personal. Others involve a whole church that is seriously divided. Some are disputes over moral standards, others over doctrine, and still others over worship practices. Some conflicts are widespread, affecting more than one church, and in some congregations there are multiple conflicts. The same conflict appears in more than one New Testament writing. Sometimes a rift is described in one text and an apparent reconciliation in another. Some passages lay down instructions for dealing with conflict, while others describe events that, surprisingly, do not conform to those instructions. *These complexities do not yield to an easy reductionism.* A careful search through the New Testament leads to the discovery of a rich diversity of relevant passages. Our first task, then, is not just to discover what is there (since it is all "hiding in plain sight"), but to organize and clarify the abundant

---

1. The authorship of Ephesians remains disputed in New Testament studies.

material. When that has been accomplished, we will explore its implications for church conflicts in the present day.

We have reached one important conclusion: if we want our response to a church conflict to be scriptural, we will have many options available. In the pages that follow, we begin with a distinction between broad principles for peace in the churches and practical instructions or steps for handling strife. We then make a further distinction between those practical steps that are general and those that arise out of contextually specific conflicts. It is these latter conflicts that we are mainly interested in, because they help us answer the question, "What did the New Testament Christians actually do instead of Matthew 18:15–17?" We then list and describe several conflict response strategies that appear in the New Testament. In each case we cite at least one example, and we briefly discuss the issue of its current relevance. Because there are often extensive scriptural quotations, we set off much of it with a label such as, "Additional scriptures and comments."

We end with a brief summary and some conclusions.

CHAPTER 1

Preliminary Distinctions and Examples

There are numerous aphorisms and admonitions in the New Testament about how followers of Jesus should relate to one another. For example, there is a multitude of sayings about church members being at peace, being unified, loving one another, bearing one another's burdens, and so forth. Indeed, there are too many to cite here. Yet most of these references give no specific guidance about how peace or unity is to be attained. Certainly there are appeals to live in the Spirit, to follow Christ as head of the church, and similar theological statements, and these broad principles may be summed up in the rule of love. This is, of course, the essential foundation for the specific instructions on handling conflict that we find throughout the New Testament. But this inspired counsel is not procedural. Other more detailed texts build on that foundation, and those practical instructions are the material we will explore in the coming chapters.

When it comes to the level of more specific instructions on handling church strife, we have a further problem. All of these texts are responding to particular situations within limiting historical and cultural contexts. Ignoring these contexts means that such passages are often applied inappropriately today. When we study these local conflict situations, we discover that New Testament churches and writers were not following the teaching in Matthew 18:15–17, if they knew about it,[1] and sometimes did not even follow other general, foundational guidelines.

To deal with a church conflict today using the guidance of the Bible does not mean assigning these texts arbitrarily to the cases at hand. One cannot, with scriptural integrity, prioritize one passage and ignore all the other potentially relevant texts. Nor can one take an instruction that pertains to a specific, local conflict and automatically impose it on a current case in a very different context.

We begin by taking a first look at several texts that stand out because they seem to give specific instructions that, at first glance, appear to be *the* method for conflict management or, at least *the initial* steps that must be taken. Taken out of context, any of these passages, if used as an exclusive or global mandate, would close the reader's mind to other important possibilities.

We will visit these passages now, out of context, and see them again in the chapters that follow within their broader context.

MATTHEW 5:23–26

> So when you are offering your gift at the altar, if you remember that your brother or sister has something against you, leave your gift there before the altar and go; first be reconciled to your brother or sister, and then come and offer your gift. Come to terms quickly with your accuser while you are on the way to court with him, or your accuser may hand you over to the judge, and the judge to the guard, and you will be thrown into prison.

1. It remains problematic that this passage is unique to Matthew's gospel, contains the word "church," when no such churches yet existed, and may well reflect a *post-resurrection* teaching of Jesus, finally written down about 80 C.E., when the Gospel of Matthew was published. How widely was this Matthean teaching about conflict known among other early Christian leaders and their converts' churches? Apparently not widely enough to have become the normative practice, as is often assumed today.

> Truly I tell you, you will never get out until you have paid
> the last penny.

It does not appear that a specific conflict is in view here. The situation is hypothetical ("if you remember"), but it does allude to what must have been a common experience in Jesus' lifetime. Someone is offering a sacrifice at the altar in the Temple and remembers that another person has something against him or her. The nature of the conflict is personal. The trouble is between two people who are part of the same community. This text addresses the person who has been accused and may or may not be guilty.

There are three potential results from this conflict. The first is reconciliation, the preferred result. The second is a negotiated settlement, expressed in the injunction to "come to terms" with the accuser. The last, and least favored, is judgment by a third party who acts with authority and exacts punishment.

MATTHEW 18:15-17

> If another member of the church sins against you, go and
> point out the fault when the two of you are alone. If the
> member listens to you, you have regained that one. But
> if you are not listened to, take one or two others along
> with you, so that every word may be confirmed by the
> evidence of two or three witnesses. If the member refuses
> to listen to them, tell it to the church; and if the offender
> refuses to listen even to the church, let such a one be to
> you as a Gentile and a tax collector.

Here the conflict is also personal, as in Matthew 5:23–26. But it is a dispute between two members of a Christian community and potentially disruptive. While the previous example addressed the accused person, this example addresses the accuser. The Gospel author is aware of the church as a body with procedures for order and discipline. The situation, again, does not refer to a specific dispute, but raises a hypothetical situation.

There are three possible results: the matter is settled face to face, the matter is settled within a small group, or the matter is settled by the judgment of the church as a body. Some suggest that "let such a one be to you as a Gentile and a tax collector" requires the offer of redemption and fellowship, as Jesus himself offered to tax collectors and sinners. Others see in this the authority of the church to decide who may be a member in good standing.

LUKE 17:3–5

> Be on your guard! If another disciple sins, you must rebuke the offender, and if there is repentance, you must forgive. And if the same person sins against you seven times a day, and turns back to you seven times and says, "I repent," you must forgive. The apostles said to the Lord, "Increase our faith!"

Luke may be conflating two sayings of Jesus that are treated separately in Matthew,[2] one concerns how to respond when another disciple offends (sins against) and the other calling for repeated forgiveness. Jesus, in Luke's account, warns the disciples to be on their guard against sin, and to confront it in the other. But the next sentence either clarifies with "sins against you," or functions as an independent and separate saying. Where Matthew refers to the offended person pointing out the fault, Luke uses a stronger term, "rebuke" the offender. Where Matthew refers to the offender listening, Luke uses "repents." As in Matthew the case is hypothetical, but the resolution has but one option: forgiveness. All of the action to resolve the conflict is individual. There is no sense of the church or a larger community being involved.

ROMANS 16:17–18

> I urge you, brothers and sisters, to keep an eye on those who cause dissensions and offenses, in opposition to the teaching that you have learned; avoid them. For such people do not serve our Lord Christ, but their own

---

2. Not that Luke used Matthew in composing his Gospel. He may, however, have known the same sayings of Jesus.

appetites, and by smooth talk and flattery they deceive the hearts of the simple-minded.

The conflict is general and concerns false teaching and wrong values. Those persons about whom Paul is concerned not only oppose the teaching that the Romans had learned, but they do so in a way that causes dissensions and offenses. The term "offenses," along with the reference to "their own appetites," may imply that the false teaching was about morality. Paul instructs his readers to keep an eye on such people and to avoid them. There is no confrontation, rebuke, correction, or any other direct action suggested.

1 CORINTHIANS 5

Although conflicts within the Corinthian congregation are well-documented in Paul's letters, there are two situations where the *lack* of conflict rather than the presence of conflict is the problem as Paul sees it. First Corinthians 5 refers to a serious moral offense occurring, yet the Corinthians are arrogant about it. They are boasting (v. 6), evidently about their moral "freedom."

Paul puts himself at odds with the person who is committing the offense. He has already passed judgment on him. There is the conflict, and it is "settled" unilaterally by Paul's judgment.

Further, Paul puts himself at odds with the Corinthians as a whole. He tells them what they should feel: sorrow ("Should you not rather have mourned . . . ?" v. 2). He tells them what they should do: evict the offender from the congregation and "hand this man over to Satan" (v. 5). They should not associate with such persons, or with others who violate the norms of sexual morality or who are greedy, idolaters, revilers, drunks or robbers. "Do not even eat with such a one" (v. 11). Thus he provokes and urges the Corinthians to enter into conflict with such offenders, and to shun them.

1 CORINTHIANS 6:1-8:

When any of you has a grievance against another, do you dare to take it to court before the unrighteous, instead of taking it before the saints? Do you not know that the saints will judge the world? And if the world is to be judged by you, are you incompetent to try trivial cases? Do you not know that we are to judge angels—to say nothing of ordinary matters? If you have ordinary cases, then, do you appoint as judges those who have no standing in the church? I say this to your shame. Can it be that there is no one among you wise enough to decide between one believer and another, but a believer goes to court against a believer—and before unbelievers at that? In fact, to have lawsuits at all with one another is already a defeat for you. Why not rather be wronged? Why not rather be defrauded? But you yourselves wrong and defraud—and believers at that.

Here the offended person has three options: a civil lawsuit, arbitration by the church, or simply accepting the actions of the offender. There is nothing here about confronting the offender, nothing about calling witnesses, nothing about punishment, nothing even about forgiveness. Yet the previous case and this one are similar. Both passages deal with individual, personal conflicts. Both deal with an offenders and victims. Neither involves church doctrine, worship practices, or anything that would seem to directly affect the church as an organization.

1 CORINTHIANS 11:17-34

A similar case is found in 1 Corinthians 11. The presenting issue is the Lord's Supper. The underlying problem is divisions and factions in the church (1:10—3:23). Someone in the church has brought this problem to Paul's attention, but most of the Corinthians were not very concerned about the situation. On the one hand, the level of the conflict is low, because the Corinthians appear quite happy in their factions and with eating (and even getting drunk) separately without waiting for one another (v. 21). But that was not good news from Paul's perspective; he saw their behavior as a sign of divisions that ultimately threaten the church. On the other hand, the conflict is higher in level, because it was important enough for some members to contact Paul and for him to respond.

Paul responds to this divisiveness by instructing them concerning the Lord's Supper and how to receive it in a worthy manner.

> Examine yourselves, and only then eat of the bread and drink of the cup . . . So, then, my brothers and sisters, when you come together to eat, wait for one another. If you are hungry, eat at home, so that when you come together, it will not be for your condemnation (11:28, 33–34).

He puts a positive spin on their factions (v. 19), and then tells them to resolve the conflict by self-examination and by establishing more orderly procedures for observing the Lord's Supper. The resolution of their conflicts relies on changed attitudes, a deeper understanding of the Lord's Supper, and what we might call procedural changes.

EPHESIANS 4:25–32

> So then, putting away falsehood, let all of us speak the truth to our neighbors, for we are members of one another. Be angry but do not sin; do not let the sun go down on your anger, and do not make room for the devil. Thieves must give up stealing; rather let them labor and work honestly with their own hands, so as to have something to share with the needy. Let no evil talk come out of your mouths, but only what is useful for building up, as there is need, so that your words may give grace to those who hear. And do not grieve the Holy Spirit of God, with which you were marked with a seal for the day of redemption. Put away from you all bitterness and wrath and anger and wrangling and slander, together with all malice, and be kind to one another, tender-hearted, forgiving one another, as God in Christ has forgiven you.

A major theme in the letter to the Ephesians is Christ's breaking down of the wall that separated the Jewish and Gentile believers (2:11–22). While this passage above does not give step-by-step procedures for ending conflict, it does shed light on some of the key elements in doing so. The readers are instructed to change aspects of their behavior, to deepen their spirituality, and to relate to one another in a more caring way. There is nothing here about formal actions of a church body.

PHILIPPIANS 3:2–3

Paul writes to the Philippians, "I urge Euodia and I urge Syntyche to be of the same mind in the Lord. Yes, and I ask you also, my loyal companion, help these women, for they have struggled beside me in the work of the gospel, together with Clement and the rest of my co-workers, whose names are in the book of life." While Paul advises Euodia and Syntyche to be of the same mind, he does not stop there. He urges his "loyal companion" (or "Syzygus," if the Greek word is a name) to help them. This is not much. It suggests mediation. At least we can recognize that Paul suggests a facilitation of some kind.

So far, we have not seen any consistent procedure in the New Testament for resolving conflicts among the followers of Jesus. Nor can we discern different processes for different types of conflict. The instructions are partial and situational or moral and spiritual. Matthew and Luke vary in their expression of what appears to be a saying of Jesus, and Paul's instructions vary from letter to letter and even within one letter. We shall see in what follows that whatever might seem to be general conflict management instructions in the Gospels were not followed in practice in the early churches. It could be argued that the procedures referred to in the Gospels, being written later than Paul's letters, represent another attempt to bring order out of his multivaried approach to conflict. But that, we do not know.

The New Testament provides a rich variety of accounts of conflict on all levels and shows how these conflicts were handled.

How, then, does conflict in the New Testament get resolved? If it does not get resolved, what attempts are made at resolution? It was certainly not on the basis of the instructions we have already cited. In fact, we will see that those instructions are at times contrary to actual practice.

Though there are differences between any two conflict-related passages, it is possible, nevertheless, to discern some *common* courses of action that are described in the New Testament.

For example, a procedure is described in some detail in Acts 6:1–7 where "the Hellenists" complain about their widows not being served. In fact, it appears that the apostles pronounced a decision, and the whole body of believers accepted it. Here we have the combination of an edict and a consensus. Other passages also contain other combined methods.

The task for us now is to describe and discuss a number of conflict resolution methods, i.e., specific strategies that were recognized and practiced in New Testament Christian communities. In the chapters that follow, we will, first, name and describe each method; then we will briefly discuss specific texts that refer to them.

CHAPTER 2

The Dictum

The first of these methods is the dictum. It can be defined as
a pronouncement by a recognized authority that is aimed at
settling issues and ending a dispute. It is expressed through terms
such as: command, adjure, rebuke, judge, and admonish. Our review of examples will show that the dictum was usually used (not
always) when the speaker had recognized authority and a high
intent to settle the issue or issues and less concern for the relationships between those involved in the conflict. It appears that the
dictum is used often when the speaker or writer believes that the
integrity of the church is at stake. We shall also see that the dictum
was not always successful in settling issues and ending disputes.

Nevertheless, *the dictum is the most frequently used conflict
response in the New Testament*. Often it appears as the word of an
apostle, elder, or other leader. Sometimes it is delivered with a pro-
phetic tone, as the word of the Lord. Perhaps its frequent use is a
reflection of a society where disputes are expected to be decided
by authority figures.

The use of dicta was not always successful. Paul did not
achieve his conflict resolution goals for the Corinthians without

turning to other methods. In 1 Corinthians 5, Paul, in writing to the church about a serious moral failure, said:

> For though absent in body, I am present in spirit; and as if present I have already pronounced judgment in the name of the Lord Jesus on the man who has done such a thing. When you are assembled, and my spirit is present with the power of our Lord Jesus, you are to hand this man over to Satan for the destruction of the flesh, so that his spirit may be saved in the day of the Lord . . . Clean out the old yeast . . . But now I am writing to you not to associate with anyone who bears the name of brother or sister who is sexually immoral or greedy, or is an idolater, reviler, drunkard, or robber. Do not even eat with such a one. For what have I to do with judging those outside? Is it not those who are inside that you are to judge? God will judge those outside. Drive out the wicked person from among you.

He states no concern about preserving the current relationship with the offender, no call for repentance, no openness to reconciliation. His only concern is the issue of immorality and its effect on the church. That must be resolved. Paul puts himself into conflict with the Corinthians and puts them into conflict with the offender and with anyone like him. In 2 Corinthians chapters 10–13, Paul deals extensively with conflict with false apostles. Here Paul expresses and uses a variety of methods of addressing conflict. With regard to his use of dicta, that is, his authority and power to solve conflicts, several passages, illustrated below, stand out.

In this context Paul has a strong desire to preserve his relationship with the Corinthians. These texts show how Paul tried again and again to lead the Corinthians to a better state. But his use of dicta and apostolic authority had not proved sufficient. He had written at least twice, if not three times before, and paid them several visits. He pleads with them, he mentors and teaches them, and he writes letters that are emotionally laden and aimed exclusively at building relationships beyond just solving specific problems.

He is still, however, using his authority to build them up, and in that regard he can still use dicta. This is either directly stated or implied in the following verses:

2 Corinthians 10:4–6: "for the weapons of our warfare are not merely human, but they have divine power to destroy strongholds. We destroy arguments and every proud obstacle raised up against the knowledge of God, and we take every thought captive to obey Christ. We are ready to punish every disobedience when your obedience is complete."

2 Corinthians 10:8: "Now, even if I boast a little too much of our authority, which the Lord gave for building you up and not for tearing you down, I will not be ashamed of it."

2 Corinthians 10:11: "Let such people understand that what we say by letter when absent, we will also do when present."

2 Corinthians 13:2: "I warned those who sinned previously and all the others, and I warn them now while absent, as I did when present on my second visit, that if I come again, I will not be lenient . . ."

2 Corinthians 13:10–11: "So I write these things while I am away from you, so that when I come, I may not have to be severe in using the authority that the Lord has given me for building up and not for tearing down. Finally, brothers and sisters, farewell. Put things in order, listen to my appeal, agree with one another, live in peace; and the God of love and peace will be with you."

Another example is in the Johannine Epistles. The Elder, as he calls himself (2 John 1; 3 John 1), had apparently used dicta, but his authority was rejected (1 John 2:19; 4:2, 2 John 7; 3 John 9–10), and the church remained divided. He too then turned to other methods, as we will see below.

ADDITIONAL TEXTS AND COMMENTS ABOUT THE DICTUM

There are many additional passages in the New Testament in which conflict is dealt with in an authoritative way using dicta. The following is a selection.

In Mark 14:6 and John 12:7 Jesus said, about the woman's anointing him with costly ointment, "Leave her alone" (John 12:7; "Let her alone," Mark 14:6). This is an example where the speaker, in this case Jesus, focused on the relationships in a conflict situation with his disciples.

In Acts 5:4 and 5:9, Peter rebuked Ananias and Sapphira, and they immediately died! Clearly there was no concern here for preserving relationship with them.

In Acts 8:20–23, Peter rebuked Simon Magus who wanted to purchase the gift of the Holy Spirit:

> But Peter said to him, "May your silver perish with you, because you thought you could obtain God's gift with money! You have no part or share in this, for your heart is not right before God. Repent therefore of this wickedness of yours, and pray to the Lord that, if possible, the intent of your heart may be forgiven you. For I see that you are in the gall of bitterness and the chains of wickedness."

Here is an example of some balance between dealing forcefully with a serious issue and concern for personal relationship. Simon Magus is rebuked, but his repentance will save the relationship.

In Galatians 2:11, Paul had a face-to-face confrontation in public with Peter. He later wrote about this to the Galatians, saying that he had opposed Cephas, without reporting to the Galatians what he himself said or Peter's reply. It is clear that Paul's style in this case was authoritative, accusing, and insistent. It is not clear, though, how or whether this personal conflict was actually resolved. Galatians 2:11: "But when Cephas came to Antioch, I opposed him to his face, because he stood self-condemned."

The author of the Pastoral Epistles, writing in the name of Paul, uses the phrase "turned over to Satan" as he writes to Timothy and refers to excommunication, a unilateral authoritarian action by Paul. But, it should be noted that soon after this he urges Timothy to be gentle with his flock.

1 Timothy 1:9: "By rejecting conscience, certain persons have suffered shipwreck in the faith; among them are Hymenaeus and

Alexander, whom I have turned over to Satan, so that they may learn not to blaspheme."

1 Timothy 5:20: "As for those who persist in sin, rebuke them in the presence of all, so that the rest also may stand in fear."

1 Timothy 6:11: "But as for you, man of God, shun all this; pursue righteousness, godliness, faith, love, endurance, gentleness."

The author of the Pastorals also writes similarly to Titus concerning certain people "of the circumcision" who are troubling the church: "They must be silenced" (Titus 1:11; ". . . rebuke them sharply," 1:13).

The Elder who writes the Letters of John can also use his authority and language similar to Paul's in the conflict-laden situation of the schism that has divided the Johannine community (1 John 2:19).

1 John 4:1: "Beloved, do not believe every spirit, but test the spirits to see whether they are from God; for many false prophets have gone out into the world."

1 John 5:21: "Little children, keep yourselves from idols."

2 John 7–11:

> Many deceivers have gone out into the world, those who do not confess that Jesus Christ has come in the flesh; any such person is the deceiver and the antichrist! Be on your guard, so that you do not lose what we have worked for, but may receive a full reward. Everyone who does not abide in the teaching of Christ, but goes beyond it, does not have God; whoever abides in the teaching has both the Father and the Son. Do not receive into the house or welcome anyone who comes to you and does not bring this teaching; for to welcome is to participate in the evil deeds of such a person.

3 John 9–10: "I have written something to the church; but Diotrephes, who likes to put himself first, does not acknowledge our authority. So if I come, I will call attention to what he is doing in spreading false charges against us."

John, the seer of the book of Revelation, issues authoritative dicta in conflict situations to his seven churches in the name of the risen Christ.

Revelation 2:4–5: "But I have this against you; that you have abandoned the love you had at first. Remember then from what you have fallen; repent, and do the works you did at first. If not, I will come to you and remove your lampstand from its place, unless you repent."

Revelation 2:14–16:

> But I have a few things against you: you have some there who hold to the teaching of Balaam, who taught Balak to put a stumbling block before the people of Israel, so that they would eat food sacrificed to idols and practice fornication. So you also have some who hold to the teaching of the Nicolaitans. Repent then. If not, I will come to you soon and make war against them with the sword of my mouth.

The dictum is a very frequent method for seeking to resolve personal and congregational conflict in first-century Christian communities. Most of the time, we have no idea whether the use of this practice was successful.

USING THE DICTUM IN TODAY'S CHURCH

In our time, the dictum is perhaps the least popular conflict resolution device. We live in a more egalitarian age. Most churches, even those with a hierarchical structure, are wary of power that resides in a single individual. Theologically, we are more likely to believe that the Spirit speaks through and to the community. Claims to have a word from the Lord, claims that were tested in New Testament times, are even more subject to critical evaluation today.

Is there a place for the dictum as a response to conflict within the contemporary church? It appears to be an extreme response. But perhaps there are some conflicts so damaging to the life of the church that they need to be settled unilaterally through the authoritative dictum.

The dictum can take the form of an ultimatum that brooks no contradiction; that is, that allows no further word of opposition. Alternatively, it can take the form of a ruling arrived at by an arbitrator or as the result of a case brought to an ecclesiastical panel.

In these cases, ultimatum and ruling, the issues are settled. The disputants are relieved of the burden of continuing the conflict and are denied the right to settle the issues in any other way. In the case of a ruling, the parties to the dispute have agreed to accept arbitration or to honor the appropriate church court or panel. If they have not so agreed, the issues are not really resolved; they are simply repressed.

Is there biblical warrant for this method? Clearly, there are ample examples of ultimatums and rulings within the New Testament. As a practical matter, however, the biblical evidence strongly suggests that the dictum produced little by way of genuine reconciliation.

Settling issues is one thing; reconciling disputants is another. Unless the dictum opens the pathway toward reconciliation, even its biblical warrant proves of little practical value. The work of church courts and panels, done correctly, has a good chance of resolving difficult issues while also fostering reconciliation. Ultimatums do not.

CHAPTER 3

Separation

Three somewhat different actions are included in this term. They have in common that all of them resulted in an end to the dispute process, and none of them led to reconciliation. The three actions are parting ways, shunning, and eviction from the church or excommunication.

PARTING WAYS

In Acts 15:38, we learn that John Mark had not continued with Paul and Barnabas throughout their first missionary journey. He had "deserted" them, Luke writes. As the second journey began, Paul refused to take John Mark with them. This caused a rift between Barnabas, who wanted John Mark to come along, and Paul. They went their separate ways. "The disagreement became so sharp that they parted company" (Acts 15:39). The conflict level was high and the dispute was not resolved. Later, however, there was reconciliation between Paul and John Mark,[1] as Paul writes in Colossians 4:10–11: "Aristarchus my fellow prisoner greets you, as does Mark, the cousin of Barnabas . . . And Jesus, who is called Justus greets

---

1. This assumes that it is John Mark whom Paul refers to in these passages.

you. These are the only ones of the circumcision among my co-workers for the kingdom of God, and they have been a comfort to me." And, "Epaphras, my fellow prisoner in Christ Jesus, sends greetings to you and so do Mark, Aristarchus, Demas, and Luke, my fellow workers" (Phlm 24).

While the rift involving Mark was personal, other examples involved the separation of groups from one another. In 1 John 2:19, 4:2, and 2 John 7, we read of a group leaving the church in a conflict over church teaching.

Parting ways, as described in the New Testament, had mixed results. On the one hand, it quieted the conflict and kept the door open to later reconciliation of individuals. But when the break was between groups, as in 1–3 John, the controversy was not resolved, as far as we know. Those who remained in the church took a "good riddance" attitude toward those who had left. Indeed, in retrospect, it may well have been good that they left, as belief in the incarnation of Christ was at stake. Our point remains, though: the choice to part severed the church.

In our time, parting ways is one of the most popular responses to church conflict. It is not uncommon for individuals to leave a church because of unhappiness with a pastor, church leader, or fellow member. In many cases they return after some time has passed. Sadly, we frequently see groups forming within congregations who either leave en masse, or campaign to have an entire congregation sever its relationship with a larger church body. In those cases, there is little hope of reconciliation.

We seem to have completed a cycle in the past four or five decades that saw American Protestant denominations reunited, particularly those that became divided over slavery and race. During those decades we saw great progress in the ecumenical movement. The trend lately, however, has moved to new divisions, new partings of the way. In the New Testament those divisions were over the heart of the gospel message itself. The divisions of our time are over lesser matters.

SHUNNING

In 2 Thessalonians 3:14 Paul writes, "Take note of those who do not obey what we say in this letter; have nothing to do with them, so that they may be ashamed." This is shunning. The purpose is to induce shame and a change of behavior. It would seem that a strong bond to the community is in place, for without it the shame would be shallow. There is there an implied expectation of reconciliation.

In our time, shunning is rare, even in Anabaptist circles. When it does occur, it is most often informal, rather than a planned and measured means of correction. Informal shunning is best understood as a kind of bullying and has no scriptural support. Since the effectiveness of formal shunning as a means of correction relies on the strength of the communal bond, it is questionable whether this tactic could be successful in today's churches, except perhaps among those with strong minority cultural identities, such as Amish and Old Order Mennonites. That bond has been greatly weakened by external factors such as denominationalism and urbanization. The move from a rural, relational social setting to an urban, transactional social setting makes a large difference.

EVICTION/EXCOMMUNICATION/EXPULSION

As noted above, Paul instructed the Corinthians to excommunicate the man who was involved with his father's wife (1 Cor 5:1). Thus, it was not only Paul, but also the church that was to take this action. We do not know what process was involved in doing so. Nor do we know the full effect of the required action. Did this community expulsion have its roots in the synagogue system? To be driven out of the synagogue (*aposunagōgos*) was to lose one's place in the community (John 9:22; 12:42; 16:2). It was a kind of death, religiously and socially.

Expectations of loyalty to the church are elevated during times of persecution. The Donatists demanded severity, and even expulsion, for those who had, in their view, betrayed the Christian faith and church during the persecutions of the second and third centuries. The seventeenth-century Puritans in the Massachusetts Bay Colony ousted Roger Williams and Anne Hutchinson for violating community standards. Excommunication continues to occur in our own time.[2] The use of shunning and of expulsion is different in different social contexts.

In our time, expulsion from the church may have very limited social effects. We don't live in a society where that will matter very much. We view our associations as voluntary, including our church affiliation. Theological concepts notwithstanding, we voluntarily join a church or denomination, rather than being required to belong to one, or being born into one. We "belong" in a social, membership sense. If we say that we belong to God, though, we express a profound relationship that doesn't, for most of us, carry over necessarily to the church. This view of the individual vis-a-vis the church is, of course, a reflection of our post-Enlightenment modernist mentality with its emphasis on reason and the autonomous self.

Churches rightly remove individuals from their rolls if they become inactive or move away without notice. But to do so as an act of church discipline is reserved for the most severe cases. These cases, however, do occur. The New Testament examples concern conditions that were viewed as mortal threats to the integrity of the church itself.

2. "Excommunicated persons are 'cut off from the Church,' barred from receiving the Eucharist and from taking an active part in the liturgy (reading, bringing the offerings, etc.), but they remain Catholics. They are urged to retain a relationship with the Church, as the goal is to encourage them to repent and return to active participation in its life" (John P. Beal, James A. Coriden, and Thomas J. Green, eds., *New Commentary on the Code of Canon Law* (New York: Paulist, 2000) 63 [commentary on canon 11]).

ADDITIONAL TEXTS AND COMMENTS ABOUT SEPARATION

Shunning

In Romans 16:17, Paul urges the Romans to watch, but avoid those who cause dissentions and offenses. There is nothing here about correcting, confronting, or reconciling such persons. The passage suggests a form of shunning.

Similarly in 2 Thessalonians 3:6, 14–15 Paul writes:

> Now we command you, beloved, in the name of our Lord Jesus Christ, to keep away from believers who are living in idleness and not according to the tradition that they received from us . . . Take note of those who do not obey what we say in this letter; have nothing to do with them, so that they may be ashamed. Do not regard them as enemies, but warn them as believers.

This passage from 2 Thessalonians 3 also contains two other conflict response methods: the dictum ("we command you," 3:6; "we gave you this command," 3:10; "Now such persons we command and exhort," 3:12) and mentoring (which will be discussed below; see 3:7: "you ought to imitate us," and 3:9: "in order to give you an example to imitate").

Note also Paul's use of reconciling terms such as "beloved" and "Do not regard them as enemies, but warn them as believers" (2 Thess 3:15). Thus, it is a form of separation, but not absolute as in other examples.

Also in 2 John 9–11 the Elder writes: "Everyone who does not abide in the teaching of Christ, but goes beyond it, does not have God; whoever abides in the teaching has both the Father and the Son. Do not receive into the house or welcome anyone who comes to you and does not bring this teaching; for to welcome is to participate in the evil deeds of such a person."

Hospitality was crucial for travel in the ancient world. Here, the Elder forbids such hospitality toward those who advocate false teaching, presumably the teaching that Jesus Christ did not come in the flesh (1 John 4:2; 2 John 7). In effect he urges shunning of such Christians.

The author of the Pastoral Epistles tells Titus to "have nothing more to do with anyone who causes divisions" (Titus 3:10). And, to Timothy he writes about "Hymenaeus and Alexander, whom I have turned over to Satan, so that they may learn not to blaspheme" (1 Tim 1:20).

Eviction

In 1 John the writer alludes to a conflict that resulted in a division in the Johannine community (2:19). This conflict was about the Elder's teaching, and those who went out are regarded as liars and antichrists: "Who is the liar but the one who denies that Jesus is the Christ?" (2:22). And, "[M]any antichrists have come . . ." (2:18). "They went out from us" (2:19).

The solutions to this problem were separation (in this case the false prophet "antichrists" have left the community, 4:1), testing the spirits (4:1), maintaining faith in Jesus Christ and loving one another (3:23). The level of the conflict was high, since it resulted in a schism. To what extent this may also have been an eviction of the false teachers, we do not know.

Second John cites the same conflict, this time calling the secessionists antichrists and "deceivers who have gone out into the world" (2 John 7). The Elder calls the church to love one another and to be on their guard against such people (2 John 8). He further urges them to withdraw hospitality from such false teachers (2 John 10–11).

Here the stakes are very high, and the danger is very great. The consequence of the conflict is a necessary separation. While it appears that this conflict is now between the Johannine community and an outside group, in fact those who oppose the Elder and his teaching had their roots in the community. Second John portrays the state of conflict after it has resulted in a break. He is reinforcing the central christological teaching of the church and its character as a community of mutual love.

In Third John, one of the Johannine house-churches, led by one Diotrephes, is excommunicating its members if they give support to the Elder's traveling representatives, "the brothers" (3 John 10).

Jude speaks of "intruders" (Jude 4). He calls them "blemishes on your love feasts" (Jude 12). Were they within the congregation, making this an internal conflict? In any case, they were "causing divisions" (Jude 19). Jude's prescription is exclusively about the spiritual practices that the church must do to immunize themselves to these intruders and their corrupt values. "But you, beloved, build yourselves up on your most holy faith; pray in the Holy Spirit; keep yourselves in the love of God; look forward to the mercy of our Lord Jesus Christ that leads to eternal life."

In relation to others, he counsels to have mercy on the wavering, saving others as though snatching them out of the fire, and having mercy on still others who have fallen prey to these false teachers (22–23), but no prescription is given with how to expel and exclude the intruders who "pervert the grace of our God into licentiousness and deny our only Master and Lord, Jesus Christ" (Jude 4).

In the book of Revelation John the seer makes a clear separation in the church of Thyatira between those who participate in the evils of Jezebel and "the rest of you." Some in the church were tolerating "that woman Jezebel, who calls herself a prophet and is teaching and beguiling my servants to practice fornication and to eat food sacrificed to idols" (Rev 2:20).

But the rest of the believers there, who rejected this teaching, are told to stand fast in their faith until the return of Christ (2:24–25). But again as in Jude, no mechanism is stated for dealing organizationally with the false teachers.

USING SEPARATION IN TODAY'S CHURCH

Is there a legitimate place in the contemporary church for separation as a response to conflict? How high on the list of core values for the church is unity? Are there issues before the present-day church with all of its variety that represent a threat to its existence and for which there is no alternative but separation or schism?

Not all examples of separation in the New Testament were permanent divisions, but some were. Separation in some cases meant physical distance and in other cases the severing of communication. In both forms there were mixed results. Physical distance, it appears, was more readily overcome than was a break in communication. Paul, Barnabas, and John Mark eventually reconciled, but Paul and the Christian Pharisees (Judaizers) did not.

As a practical matter, separation in the church of our time puts an end to the dynamics of conflict. It brings to a full stop not only the strife, but also any work toward reconciliation that might have been underway or possible and any work to resolve issues.

The New Testament guidance requires a careful assessment of the issues at stake, the relationships in danger, and the potential damage that separation can cause. At best separation should be temporary with the hope of restored unity clearly in view.

CHAPTER 4

Avoidance

There is some inescapable complexity when we approach the topic of avoidance. There is a clear and important difference between avoiding certain people and avoiding certain circumstances. Avoiding conflict falls in the latter category. But first let us consider the situation of avoiding certain people.

We have already discussed an aspect of this category under the heading, "Separation." We have acknowledged parting ways, shunning, and expulsion. There remains another, somewhat elusive, sense in which the New Testament calls for conflict to be responded to by staying away from certain people. In those references, the people to be avoided remain within the congregation and are not being specifically disciplined. They are, however, creating an unhealthy atmosphere, and one should not get involved with them.

Conflict avoidance appears in the New Testament in three forms: declining to participate in quarrels or arguments; passivity, that is, the plain acceptance of personal offense; and mutual forbearance or the willingness to agree to disagree.

NON-PARTICIPATION

Recognizing that "bitterness and wrath and anger and wrangling and slander together with . . . malice" (Eph 4:31) were present in the church at Ephesus, the writer calls upon the members to put away with those things. "Be angry, but do not sin; do not let the sun go down on your anger" (Eph 4:26).

PASSIVITY

Passivity is the decision to accept wrong treatment without retaliation, thus avoiding conflict. Jesus urged his followers to turn the other cheek. Paul reinforced this to the Corinthians, "Why not rather be wronged? Why not rather be defrauded?" (1 Cor 6:7).

While we think that we live in a litigious society, the Corinthians did also. The impulse to make a "big deal" out of every offense impairs churches all too often. The alternative is not to deny that the offense has occurred, but rather to accept it along with its negative consequences and move on.

MUTUAL FORBEARANCE

We might define mutual forbearance as the decision to allow differences to exist without strife. For example, in James 4:10–12, we read:

> Humble yourselves before the Lord, and he will lift you up in honor. Don't speak evil against each other, dear brothers and sisters. If you criticize and judge each other, then you are criticizing and judging God's law. But your job is to obey the law, not to judge whether it applies to you. God alone, who gave the law, is the Judge. He alone has the power to save or to destroy. So what right do you have to judge your neighbor?

Mutual forbearance is a middle ground. It neither denies the existence of disagreements nor raises them to the level of strife. Paul also addresses this model in Romans 14:5–7:

Some judge one day to be better than another, while others judge all days to be alike. Let all be fully convinced in their own minds. Those who observe the day, observe it in honor of the Lord. Also those who eat, eat in honor of the Lord, since they give thanks to God; while those who abstain, abstain in honor of the Lord and give thanks to God. We do not live to ourselves, and we do not die to ourselves.

In our experience, avoidance is the number one preferred response to church conflict, and there appears to be scriptural support for it. However, the avoidance response that operates in many contemporary cases does not always match the biblical model. The difference is that one party ignores the conflict, while the other acknowledges and deals with it. Failure to address conflict effectively, when it appears, results in festering and growing strife that gets ever more difficult to resolve.

In 2 Timothy 2:16–17a, the author of this letter urges Timothy to "avoid profane chatter for it will lead people into more and more impiety, and their talk will spread like gangrene." He further urges them in 2 Tim 2:23–25a to "[h]ave nothing to do with stupid and senseless controversies; you know that they breed quarrels. And the Lord's servant must not be quarrelsome but kindly to everyone, an apt teacher, patient, correcting opponents with gentleness."

Conflict gets ignored in part because of a belief that it should never occur in a church. If it does occur, it casts a negative light on church leadership and on the congregation. It undercuts the church's message of peace and love. It is ignored also because church leaders don't know what to do with it other than try to stifle it. While there are some who have a "morbid craving for controversy" (1 Tim 6:4), there are many who have a morbid *fear* of controversy.

Another response to conflict is the assertion that controversy is normal or even desirable. It leads to creativity by bringing out all points of view. Thus, when conflict arises, there is little reason, some say, to intervene unless it rises to a destructive level.

There is little biblical support for this viewpoint. The closest we come to this view is in 1 Corinthians 11:19: "Indeed, there have to be factions among you, for only so will it become clear who among you are genuine." Yet even here, as elsewhere, the conflict must be put on a trajectory toward resolution by one means or another. In the Pastoral Epistles the instructions to Timothy and Titus urge that church leaders have a particular duty to take the initiative in dealing with all conflict.

FORGIVING

Forgiving is a mandate, not a process. A number of good processes for apology and forgiveness have been devised. The command of Jesus to forgive seventy-seven times (Matt 18:22) has been mis-used by some as a way to keep vulnerable people, mainly women and children, in abusive relationships. Forgiving does not obligate a victim to continue to accept and endure abuse.

ADDITIONAL TEXTS AND COMMENTS ABOUT AVOIDANCE

Jesus also told his hearers to avoid conflict by first looking to their own faults before addressing the faults of others (Matt 7:3–5; Luke 6:41–42). On one occasion when Jesus' disciples had been in con-flict, arguing over who was the greatest among them, Jesus coun-seled them to be servants of one another and to consider oneself the least of all (Mark 9:35; 10:43; Luke 9:48).

In Romans 12, Paul addressed relationships within the con-gregation. He urged them to "Live in harmony with one another" (v. 16a), to practice humility ("do not be haughty, but associate with the lowly," v. 16b), and to avoid causing conflict.

He also urges them "not repay anyone evil for evil, but take thought for what is noble in the sight of all. If it is possible, so far as it depends on you, live peaceably with all. Beloved, never avenge yourselves, but leave room for the wrath of God; for it is written, 'Vengeance is mine, I will repay, says the Lord'" (12:17–19).

Instead of merely avoiding conflict, Paul advised the Roman Christians to care for their enemies ("feed them" and "give them something to drink," v. 20). The offended party should avoid conflict unilaterally.

Similarly in Romans 13:13, Paul described the way of life for followers of Jesus. They must "live honorably," avoiding "quarreling and jealousy." And the Roman Christians were not to "quarrel over opinions" (14:1). There should be no despising or passing judgment on each other (14:3–4).

Paul urged the Corinthians not to bring lawsuits against each other, but rather to be wronged or defrauded if necessary (1 Cor. 6:7).

The Corinthians are not to misuse their freedom in Christ and to flaunt their liberty in a way that is spiritually harmful to others Christians, who do not yet feel quite so free about what they eat (1 Cor 8:9–13).

In the letter to the Philippians, Paul urges them to "be of the same mind, having the same love, being in full accord and of one mind" (2:2). Specifically, he urges Euodia and Syntyche "to be of the same mind in the Lord" and eschew conflict (4:2). Paul's warning in 3:2 "to beware of the dogs, beware of the evil worker" is also counsel to avoid conflict.

In 1 Timothy the author teaches that bishops should be men who are temperate, sensible, gentle, and not quarrelsome (3:2–3). Timothy's church contained some people who had "a morbid craving for controversy and for disputes about words" (6:4). Such a mindset causes "envy, dissension, slander, base suspicions, and wrangling . . ." (6:4–5). In this situation Timothy is instructed to "shun all this" (6:11), to avoid such people who cause conflict.

In 2 Timothy 2:14, Timothy is urged to "avoid wrangling over words which does no good" and to "avoid profane chatter" (2:16) which also causes dissension and impiety. Hymenaeus and Philetus are upsetting the faith of some (2:17–18). In 2 Timothy 2:23–25a the writer reinforces what he said in 1 Timothy: "Have nothing to do with stupid and senseless controversies; you know that they breed quarrels. And the Lord's servant must not be quarrelsome but kindly to everyone, an apt teacher, patient, correcting opponents with gentleness."

Here the author is concerned about relationships and urges conflict avoidance and a hope for reconciliation.

Titus 3:2–3 is similar. Titus's Cretans ("always liars, vicious brutes, lazy gluttons," 1:12) are: "to speak evil of no one, to avoid quarreling, to be gentle, and to show every courtesy to everyone. For we ourselves were once foolish, disobedient, led astray, slaves to various passions and pleasures, passing our days in malice and envy, despicable, hating one another."

And like Timothy, Titus must "avoid stupid controversies, genealogies, dissensions, and quarrels about the law, for they are unprofitable and worthless. After a first and second admonition, have nothing more to do with anyone who causes divisions" (3:9–10).

James makes note of "conflicts and disputes" among his readers (4:1–2). He points out the cause as selfish desire. What is needed is separation from the "world" (4:4), resisting the devil (4:7), drawing near to God (4:8), and humility (4:10). They are not to "speak evil against one other" (4:11) and are not to "grumble against one another" (5:9).

All these are counsels to avoid conflict.

USING AVOIDANCE IN TODAY'S CHURCH

Is avoidance of conflict a realistic possibility in our time? Is it not the case that some conflict is inevitable as the New Testament material seems to demonstrate?

The present irony is that, on the one hand, there are volumes of writings about church conflict and what to do with it and cadres of consultants to assist in dealing with church conflict, while, on the other hand, there are unrelenting calls to avoid conflict and to prevent it from ever happening.

In practice, churches today prefer avoidance to any other conflict response. That approach, if it turns a blind eye to conflict, does nothing to promote the peace and unity of the church, and ends in failure.

Nevertheless, in one sense, there is a place for avoidance. In fact, much of the biblical material insists on it. The correct and practical avoidance approach is to (1) acknowledge the conflict (and in that sense not avoid it), (2) give it full recognition as part of the life of the church, and (3) refuse to engage in its negative drama and dynamics.

This kind of avoidance focuses on the relationships between those who are in conflict, giving the restoration or maintenance of those relationships full and exclusive attention. It does nothing, however, to directly resolve the issues that caused the relationship disruption.

CHAPTER 5

Teaching and Mentoring

Teaching fills the pages of the New Testament. Our focus is on teaching that is aimed at dealing with specific conflicts. Mentoring, on the other hand, is training through using one's self as an example. We find indications of mentoring when Paul, for example, uses the phrase, "be imitators of me [us]" (1 Cor 4:16; 11:1; Eph 5:1; Phil 3:17; 1 Thess 1:16; 2 Thess 3:7, 9).

Paul's well-known metaphor of "one body" for the church (Rom 12:4–5; 1 Cor 12:12–31) serves as an example of effective teaching and mutual forbearance. This counsel on how to handle conflict in the Corinthian situation was part of Paul's persuasion strategy to promote peace and unity in that congregation.

Paul not only gave a metaphor through which his readers could reposition themselves away from thinking of themselves as from Jewish or Gentile origin toward being united organically, but he did so in a way that honored both traditions, obviating the need to choose between them. All members of the church body in Rome or Corinth could see themselves as important to the life and work of the whole congregation, with each member's giftedness playing an important role.

In 2 Thessalonians 3:7–9, Paul offers himself and his colleagues in ministry as examples to imitate. He had avoided conflict in Thessalonica by setting aside his own rights and doing what he thought was best for the church. "For you, yourselves know how you ought to imitate us; we were not idle when we were with you, and we did not eat anyone's bread without paying for it; but with toil and labor we worked night and day, so that we might not burden any of you. This was not because we do not have that right, but in order to give you an example to imitate."

REFRAMING

One very helpful way of teaching is reframing. Reframing might be understood as teaching that is directed toward handling conflict by suggesting a context, or frame, within which a new understanding might occur and which might then make reconciliation more likely. In conflict management and mediation there is often confusion between restating and reframing. Restating is giving feedback in different terms. "She's a liar," is restated as "You haven't felt that you could always trust her." It is used to soften a statement, lower tension, and enhance the dialogue. Reframing, however, is placing the conflict within a new context in such a way that the parties can reexamine their viewpoints, attitudes, and behaviors. In the New Testament texts on conflict that follow we note this technique of reframing.

In Matthew 5:43–45 Jesus says, "love your enemies." He then gives teaching that positions his hearers as children of God who see God blessing and helping God's own enemies. "You have heard that it was said, 'You shall love your neighbor and hate your enemy.' But I say to you, Love your enemies and pray for those who persecute you, so that you may be children of your Father in heaven; for he makes his sun rise on the evil and on the good, and sends rain on the righteous and on the unrighteous."

Similarly, in Mark 10:42–45 (cf. Matt 20:25–28) Jesus calls on his disciples to be servants to one another and then reframes his followers as those who have been served and ransomed by the glorious Son of Man.

> So Jesus called them and said to them, "You know that among the Gentiles those whom they recognize as their rulers lord it over them, and their great ones are tyrants over them. But it is not so among you; but whoever wishes to become great among you must be your servant, and whoever wishes to be first among you must be slave of all. For the Son of Man came not to be served but to serve, and to give his life a ransom for many."

Luke's Gospel (22:24–27) puts it differently, emphasizing Jesus as their reframed paradigmatic example of service, and deemphasizing the tyrannical nature of the Roman rulers.

> A dispute also arose among them as to which one of them was to be regarded as the greatest. But he said to them, "The kings of the Gentiles lord it over them; and those in authority over them are called benefactors. But not so with you; rather the greatest among you must become like the youngest and the leader like one who serves. For who is greater, the one who is at the table or the one who serves? Is it not the one at the table? But I am among you as one who serve."

Today, teaching about conflict management and mentoring by example are sadly lacking. Some universities offer conflict management courses (and some of these are even available online, e.g., at MIT and Notre Dame), but seminaries are often deficient in this regard. There is a significant church conflict management history and practice that includes a body of literature and many experienced consultants. But, for the most part, these exist outside the official ecclesiastical structures. They lack a professional organization, with universally accepted standards of competence, ethics, and accountability. Pastors and church lay leaders receive little training in this area, which helps explain the strong tendency for many of them to ignore conflict and to hope it will simply go away.

ADDITIONAL TEXTS AND COMMENTS ABOUT TEACHING AND MENTORING

In Romans 11:13–24 Paul seeks to defuse the potential arrogance and conflict between the Gentile Christians in Rome and their Jewish neighbors who have not yet believed in Jesus. He urges them to consider that they, the Gentiles, have been grafted into the tree of Israel, and he warns them that they only remain by God's grace and their faith. He also wants them to share his hope that God's people, the Jews, will turn and be reconciled to God.

In Romans 11:30–32, Paul appeals to these Gentile Christians to recognize that all are saved only by God's mercy extended to all people. "Just as you were once disobedient to God but have now received mercy because of their disobedience, so they have now been disobedient in order that, by the mercy shown to you, they too may now receive mercy. For God has imprisoned all in disobedience so that he may be merciful to all."

Likewise in Romans 14:10–11, Paul teaches against passing judgment or despising one another, in that, "We will all stand before the judgment seat of God" (14:10). This places Jew and Gentile Christians in the same position. "Why do you pass judgment on your brother or sister? Or you, why do you despise your brother or sister? For we will all stand before the judgment seat of God. For it is written, 'As I live, says the Lord, every knee shall bow to me, and every tongue shall give praise to God.'"

In Romans 15 Paul urges mutual forbearance and calls for pleasing one's neighbor rather than seeking to please oneself, on the grounds that "Christ did not please himself" (15:3). Paul prays that God, whose nature is steadfastness and encouragement, will grant the Roman Christians "to live in harmony with one another" (15:5) in order that "together you may with one voice glorify the God and Father of our Lord Jesus Christ" (15:6).

He urges Gentile and Jewish Christians in Rome to "[w]elcome one another, therefore, just as Christ has welcomed you" (15:7). In fact, Paul says, Christ became a servant of the Jewish people "that he might confirm the promises given to the patriarchs, and in order that the Gentiles might glorify God for his mercy" (15:8–9). Thus, Paul again puts the two groups together in the same context.

Similarly in 1 Corinthians 4:3–5, addressing the conflict in Corinth over the veneration of certain human teachers, such as Paul, Apollos, and Peter, Paul reminds them that God is the one to whom these teachers are ultimately accountable, not to the Corinthians.

> But with me it is a very small thing that I should be judged by you or by any human court. I do not even judge myself. I am not aware of anything against myself, but I am not thereby acquitted. It is the Lord who judges me. Therefore do not pronounce judgment before the time, before the Lord comes, who will bring to light the things now hidden in darkness and will disclose the purposes of the heart. Then each one will receive commendation from God.

Paul teaches the struggling and conflicted Galatians that they are one in Christ. In Galatians 5:6 he says, "For in Christ Jesus neither circumcision nor uncircumcision counts for anything; the only thing that counts is faith working through love." The reality of being in Christ establishes a common context within which attitudes and behaviors are shaped and evaluated.

Concerned about the conflict within the congregation, Paul ends his teaching in this section (Gal 5:13–15) of the letter with these urgent and warning words,

> For you were called to freedom, brothers and sisters; only do not use your freedom as an opportunity for self-indulgence, but through love become slaves to one another. For the whole law is summed up in a single commandment, "You shall love your neighbor as yourself." If, however, you bite and devour one another, take care that you are not consumed by one another.

In Ephesians 2:14–15 the writer speaks about the historic conflict between Jews and Gentiles in early Christianity as a thing of the past. He does so by focusing the reader's gaze on Christ. "But now in Christ Jesus you who were once far off have been brought near by the blood of Christ. For he is our peace; in his flesh he has made both groups into one and has broken down the dividing wall, that is, the hostility between us. And, through him both of us have access in one Spirit to the Father."

So both Jews and Gentiles have been brought near to God by the sacrifice of Christ and have been encompassed by the peace of Christ. Teaching that keeps the risen Christ central reduces, and might even eliminate, long-standing ethnic and cultural differences.

In Philippians 3:15–17 Paul offers himself to the Philippians as an example to be imitated, as we saw above in 2 Thessalonians. Differences among congregational members can be helpfully addressed by calling to mind those who have mentored the congregation in the past and by modeling one's conduct on those mature Christian leaders: "Let those of us then who are mature be of the same mind; and if you think differently about anything, this too God will reveal to you. Only let us hold fast to what we have attained. Brothers and sisters, join in imitating me, and observe those who live according to the example you have in us."

And 1 Peter 5:3 urges congregational leaders to mentor by example: "Do not lord it over those in your charge, but be examples to the flock."

USING TEACHING AND MENTORING IN TODAY'S CHURCH

Teaching and mentoring are part of the daily work of almost every church. What role might they have in response to conflict? Good teaching transmits information in the hope of transformation, while mentoring is more about relationships and skill development. In times of conflict specific clear, helpful counsel is needed, and skills for coping and for change are required.

In practice, teaching may be given to individuals or to groups. In most contemporary congregations there are members from a wide variety of backgrounds and experiences. Sometimes those members lack knowledge about the beliefs, polity, and traditions of the church. Hence, they may have unrealistic and inappropriate expectations that give rise to conflict.

Teaching, then, as a response to conflict, may provide context-setting information about these matters in a way that helps all members move toward reconciliation. But it may also be necessary to teach about conflict itself and suggest ways such difficulties have been faced and resolved before. When an outside consultant is used, church leaders can benefit from this teaching along with everyone else.

Skills for coping with conflict and moving toward positive change can be developed through one-on-one mentoring and through other methods of training such as workshops.

As a practical matter, teaching and mentoring in the presence of conflict are ways of indirectly strengthening the church's ability to resolve issues peacefully and to maintain and restore healthy relationships.

CHAPTER 6

Negotiation

Negotiation may take many forms, but two principal ones are found in the New Testament: outright bargaining and the use of narrative that persuades. Both can be used in managing contemporary congregational conflict. Matthew 5:25 assumes negotiation and commands with some urgency coming to terms with one's adversary: "Come to terms quickly with your accuser while you are on the way to court with him, or your accuser may hand you over to the judge, and the judge to the guard, and you will be thrown into prison."

The entire Corinthian correspondence might be viewed as Paul negotiating, using many of the tactics we have described in this book, with the Corinthians for a better relationship with them. The tone is often one of conciliation, as in 2 Cor 6:11–13: "We have spoken frankly to you Corinthians; our heart is wide open to you. There is no restriction in our affections, but only in yours. In return—I speak as to children—open wide your hearts also."

The same plea for reconciliation continues in 2 Cor 7:2a: "Make room in your hearts for us." Paul then launches into a personal narrative to explain his previous conduct as a way of negotiating peace with the Corinthians (7:2b–16).

The entire letter to Philemon consists of a carefully worded negotiation between Paul and Philemon regarding Philemon's slave, Onesimus, who has now become a Christian and is being sent back to Philemon. The negotiation is necessary because Onesimus's return puts him in great jeopardy, and Paul wants to spare him punishment, which could even have included death. We see Paul's negotiating strategy when he writes, "[T]hough I am bold enough in Christ to command you to do your duty, yet I would rather appeal to you on the basis of love . . ." (vv. 8–9), and, "I wanted to keep him with me . . . but I preferred to do nothing without your consent" (vv. 13a, 14), and, "Welcome him as you would welcome me" (v. 17), and finally, "If he has wronged you in any way, or owes you anything, charge that to my account" (vv. 18–19).

Negotiation is sometimes supported by the participation of a more neutral third party, as James appears to be in Acts 15:13–21 at the Jerusalem Council. Paul and Silas, and even Peter, stated their case for more openness in early Christianity to the full inclusion of Gentiles. The Christian Pharisees opposed this. James appears as a conciliating negotiator, pronouncing the compromise solution that the assembly agreed to.

In our time, negotiation, with or without mediation, is one of the most common and most effective strategies in responding to church strife. It is widely recognized that church strife must be addressed at a spiritual level, involving a change of heart, as well as on a practical level. Achieving agreements with substantial content is often the first step toward building trust.

ADDITIONAL TEXTS AND COMMENTS ABOUT NEGOTIATION

In Acts 11, when Peter is challenged about his recent eating with Gentiles (Acts 10), his response is to reiterate the full story of his vision and the circumstances of his encounter with the Roman centurion Cornelius and his family. The intent of this narrative is both to persuade (to negotiate with) the leaders of the Jerusalem church and shows Luke's intent to persuade the implied readers of

Acts that the inclusion of the Gentiles into emerging Christianity is God's will.

Similarly in Acts 15 we hear that the whole assembly at the Jerusalem Council "kept silence, and listened to Barnabas and Paul as they told of all the signs and wonders that God had done through them among the Gentiles" (15:12). This narration was part of a strategy of negotiation that resulted in the successful (at least for the moment) inclusion of the Gentiles into the emerging church without the imposition of circumcision.

As Paul negotiated a reconciliation with the Corinthians, he reconstructed in 2 Corinthians 7:2–13 the narrative of their previous conflict and his own intentions. He spoke of his arrival, his previous letter, his suffering, the arrival of Titus, their repentance, their having proved themselves guiltless, and the result of comfort and joy.

In 2 Corinthians 11:22–28 Paul recites at length the narrative of his suffering for the gospel. He views this suffering as authenticating his apostleship over against attacks on him and his commission by the "super-apostles." The narrative is part of Paul's ongoing negotiation with the Corinthians over their loyalty to him and his apostolic authority.

He continues his autobiographical narrative in chapter 12, citing his mystical experiences, revelations of exceptional character, the thorn in his flesh, his sufferings, his selfless service to them and finally, his concern that he might find behavior among them (quarreling, jealousy, anger, selfishness, slander, gossip, conceit, and disorder) that he would prefer not to have to deal with when he comes to visit them.

USING NEGOTIATION IN TODAY'S CHURCH

This is one of the most effective yet least used tools for settling issues in churches. Negotiation accomplishes the most when there is a neutral, qualified third party who facilitates the process. When disputes arise, there are always specific issues involved, mixed with personality differences and emotions that tend to cloud thinking.

People engage in conflict to a large degree because they feel mistreated, misunderstood, or not heard or respected. The matter over which they were mistreated often becomes secondary. The primary complaint is that they were disrespected.

Well-conducted negotiation provides an environment in which both parties are respected. When that is in place, the parties to the dispute can begin to think clearly about what they need and what they are prepared to give. Initially, however, they often come to the table without clarity on those points. In many cases, the person who feels disrespected really only wants an apology.

Negotiation is usually viewed as a process of making a deal or coming to an agreement that settles issues. At its best, it also restores relationships in a way that makes reaching further agreements possible. From a practical point of view, the results of successful negotiation will have a long-lasting effect.

The biblical record, taken as a whole, and particularly the Christlike values involved, supports the use of negotiation in this way.

CHAPTER 7

Official Church Action

Some New Testament conflicts were settled through official actions of the church or congregation as a body. The textual evidence varies, and in some of the briefer texts a certain amount of reasonable inference is required. The corporate actions arise from two kinds of process: debate and consensus, and authoritative pronouncement agreed to by the body. We find no reference to voting. However, a reference in 1 Corinthians 2:6 suggests a corporate action taken by the majority and thus, perhaps, a vote: "This punishment by the majority is enough for such a person." These actions generally were concerned with issues that were church-defining or around core identity.

The well-known passage from Matthew 18:17 calls for a formal action: "If the member refuses to listen to them, tell it to the church; and if the offender refuses to listen even to the church, let such a one be to you as a Gentile and a tax collector."

As mentioned previously, the decision to select deacons to serve the Hellenist widows in Acts 6:1–7 was a corporate action pronounced by the leaders and consented to by the whole body.

After Peter had brought Cornelius and his family into the Christian community (Acts 10) he was criticized by some Jewish

Christians. Peter explained his actions to the "apostles and believers" (Acts 11:1), after which they endorsed his action. The reference to "apostles and believers" suggests a leadership group and a more general group of followers. Both groups heard Peter and approved the entry of Gentiles into the Christian community.

Most of Acts 15 deals with a similar hearing, explanation, and approval in relation to Paul's outreach to Gentiles. There were two phases in this case, both involving official action. In the first phase, some people of the must-be-circumcised viewpoint came from Jerusalem to Antioch and engaged in what was "no small dissension and debate" with Paul and Barnabas about their practices (Acts 15:1–2). Official action occurred when Paul and Barnabas were commissioned to take this question up with the leaders in Jerusalem.

The second phase took place in Jerusalem, where Paul made his case to "the apostles and the elders" (Acts 15:2, 4). A decision was reached by the apostles, elders, and the whole body by consent: "Then the apostles and the elders, with the consent of the whole church, decided to choose men from among their members and to send them to Antioch with Paul and Barnabas" (Acts 15:22).

In our time, the readiness for church bodies to take action on contested issues varies greatly. Mainline denominations have suffered serious losses in part because they have taken such actions. Although those actions settled the issues, they did not repair or sustain relationships; those who strongly disagreed with the church body simply left. When it comes to contentious policy questions, a majority vote in a ruling body does not appear to be an effective strategy.

ADDITIONAL TEXTS AND COMMENTS ABOUT OFFICIAL CHURCH ACTION

Acts 21:17–26 references Paul meeting again with "the brothers," James, and "all the elders" (Acts 21:17–18). After Paul related his success in winning Gentiles for the gospel, the assembled church body was thankful for Paul's work and urged him to take measures to reassure the Jews in Jerusalem of his "orthopraxy" (Acts 21:21–24). The Jerusalem church continued to express its support for the Gentile converts along the lines of the earlier Jerusalem Council in Acts 15.

In 1 Corinthians 5:13 Paul gives strict instruction for the church as a body to drive out an evil person. This would require official, corporate action.

In 1 Corinthians 6:1–5 Paul suggests to the Corinthians that they can find within the church wise people capable of deciding between two members in conflict, rather than those members going to the local courts. This evokes the idea of a church tribunal of some kind.

In 1 Corinthians 11–14 Paul urges the church to bring order to their celebration of the Lord's Supper and other aspects of worship, actions which would be taken by the whole body.

USING OFFICIAL CHURCH ACTION IN TODAY'S CHURCH

Is it not enough that church bodies create the matrix within which the church functions? Under what conditions and in what ways do church bodies deal directly with conflict?

Conflicts in churches generally move up the organizational ladder from more specific venues to more general judicatorial bodies. In doing so, they may also broaden from specific problems to more general topics and identify potential resources and solutions. When a higher body is involved, more eyes are on the problem.

When action becomes official, it does so because previous efforts at a lower level have failed. Officials need to, and usually are able to, consider a wide range of options. Often combinations of conflict responses are required. The greatest danger comes from inaction. Officials at higher levels also can be proactive, instead of waiting for a conflict to be referred to them. They can intervene on their own initiative when necessary.

Higher-level bodies or officials also have options that do not exist at lower levels such as imposing personnel changes, directing lower bodies to take specified remedial actions, implementing facilitated mediation, and others responses.

As a practical matter, sometimes church officials can achieve conflict reduction or resolution that cannot be accomplished any other way. And there is biblical warrant for them so to act.

CHAPTER 8

Practical Summary

The first-century historical, social, and cultural context of the New Testament communities shaped the content and relational dynamics of their conflicts and their responses in practical ways. That context included the challenge of joining Jews and Gentiles in one religious community, coping with Roman persecution, distinguishing Christian beliefs and practices from paganism, and dealing with the intellectual world of Greek philosophy, particularly as it came to be played out in emerging Docetism and Gnosticism.

Today's churches live in a very different social and cultural world. They face a different set of practical challenges. They include consumerism, a wide diversity of historic and new Christian communities, and a popular mindset that is influenced by post-Enlightenment modernism.

These, and other contextual factors, such as class, race, gender and sexual orientation, influence church leaders' and members' thinking about individual freedom, local autonomy, self-reliance, appropriate association, and governing authority. This modern mindset affects how conflicts in churches arise and how they can be managed.

Our study of the New Testament texts that speak to strife within early Christian communities leads to the firm conclusion that a pragmatic, rather than ideological or dogmatic, approach to contemporary church disputes is in order and long overdue. Church leaders who bear the burden of handling conflicts can find a variety of biblical approaches that can work in their particular contexts. It is not the case that Matthew 18:15–17 is their only scriptural resource.

This pragmatic approach requires clarity about the hierarchy of core values that informs Christian practice. Our view is that the highest core values are fidelity to the gospel and love for one another. Near the top of that hierarchy are also the peace and unity of the church. Faithfulness to Jesus Christ as Savior and Lord, sacrificial love for one another, and prioritizing community peace and unity are ideals that can work together and need not be pitted against one another. In rare cases will loyalty to Christ jeopardize church unity, especially if the people involved are committed to love and listen to one another.

Beyond that, a wide range of practical measures is available. They can be used individually, sequentially, concurrently, or by trial and error. But, persistent, dedicated effort to resolve conflict is required.

Conflict management in the church needs to aim at two equal goals: the peaceful settlement of important issues and the nurture of right relationships among church members. Some of the available methods we have noted from the New Testament emphasize one of those goals, and some emphasize the other.

Our counsel is to be creative, be planful, and be pragmatic in the use of these biblical methods and models.

Conflict looks different to each person involved in it. For our purpose, it is important to attend to how the conflict might appear to a person who is not originally a part of it, but comes to it either as an authority figure or a neutral facilitator. How does the conflict look to a judicatory leader, for example, or a consultant? That person is faced with the decision to do nothing, or to do something, and if something, what to do.

In broad strokes, such a person makes an evaluation of the conflict. We would suggest two key questions: Is the conflict communal or personal? And, is the conflict damaging or moderate? This gives us four possibilities and some guidance about how one might proceed. Although we treat these as discrete choices, in practice they play out as continuities.

First, the conflict might be both communal and damaging. This represents a threat to the church itself. It calls for direct, strong, and effective action. The person taking that action is, however, in danger of being swept up into the conflict and must strive to escape that. It appears clear, for example, that Paul, in dealing with the Corinthians, did not maintain a position outside the conflict, but became part of it. It can be argued that this hurt his effectiveness.

Second, the conflict might be both personal and damaging. Here, individuals who need the ministry of the church are in harm's way. There is, again, a need for strong action, but this time action of a pastoral nature. There is a strong possibility that personal conflicts can spill over into the community. Containment is important.

Third, the conflict might be communal, but moderate. The response would be aimed more toward teaching and mentoring. Here, the leader strives to nurture an atmosphere in which differences are respected and decisions are made through open and fair processes.

Fourth, the conflict might be personal and moderate. Mediation, private conversation, and counseling could be an appropriate responses.

Anyone who undertakes the task of dealing with church conflict should pause to consider her or his readiness to do so and the challenge the particular situation provides.

This requires some introspection, self-understanding, and study. Everyone has strengths and limitations. The challenge here is not about one's whole personality or career; it concerns, rather, a person's ability to handle conflict, or to help others who are caught in conflict.

The person considering intervention might list his or her personal attributes that will help in working with the conflict. Drawing on previous experiences or observed events might evoke one's own abilities. For example, if others consider an individual to be a good listener, that ability is worth noting.

Further, any significant limitations that one brings to the conflict should be noted. For example, if one is easily provoked to anger, taking note of this limitation may help such persons be cautious as they undertake the healing work of resolution and reconciliation.

The formal aspects of one's role, particularly of a pastor, denominational official, or any other office need to be observed. Does it fall to that individual to deal with the conflict at hand?

By virtue of the pastoral office, or by virtue of being an officer in the church, one has been granted certain rights, powers and duties. Some of those are formally established. Others derive from long-established traditions. Spelling out the attributes of the office that will help one address the conflict at hand is important. One should include any mandates in the official role (such as the requirement to report abuse if present).

Normally one's office also limits the incumbent's options to some degree. One should carefully consider the church's written rules and procedures, including bylaws, personnel policies, standards of ethical conduct, and others. She or he should list any constraints that would limit her or his ability to address the conflict at hand. This part of the exercise is aimed at avoiding some future complaint that would undermine the reconciling work.

In order to understand the potential seriousness of the conflict, the following factors should be considered: Are there factions, and if so how organized are they? A high level of organization would mean the group meets regularly, has designated leaders and/or spokespersons, has clear ways of communicating the group's positions, has stated objectives and strategies, etc.

How rapidly must one act to resolve the problem? A conflict becomes more urgent when ultimatums have been issued, specific votes or decisions are scheduled, unpaid financial obligations are pressing, and resignations have been tendered.

How widespread is the conflict? A conflict may be very intense and urgent, yet limited to two or three individuals.

How cool or hot is the conflict? Have specific credible threats been made? Do not confuse volume or tone of voice with "cool" or "hot." The mildest points can be shouted and the direst threats can be spoken softly.

How many issues, persons, groups, and positions are involved in the conflict? How many differences in language, culture, church background, age, core value system, etc., are reflected in the divisions?

The stress level and its effects are important. For example, is the pastor sleeping normally, eating well, getting time off as needed and focusing on tasks appropriately? Functional breakdown in the pastor raises urgency and signals that pastoral care will be a high priority in the intervention. Likewise, is the board meeting regularly? Are the meetings carried out per an agenda and within a reasonable time frame?

These indicators serve both to help one decide whether or not to proceed and what strategies to employ.

When church leaders are freed from the constraints of Matthew 18:15–17 and are open to the full range of biblical examples, a number of options appear. Here are some of them.

SPIRITUAL CARE: This option encompasses many potential activities beginning with prayer for and with those in conflict. One may also take steps to remind church leaders and members of their unity in Christ and of their forgiveness and duty to forgive. One may also recognize grief, anger, guilt, pride, or other spiritual problems that need to be addressed directly. Spiritual care might also involve Bible study, admonition, encouragement or the exercise of spiritual disciplines such as meditation, study, fasting, silence, confession, and others.

COUNSELING: Individuals in conflict can sometimes find their way through one-to-one professional counseling.

NEGOTIATION: In lower-level conflicts, the parties can settle issues themselves through negotiation. Negotiation is appropriate when: a) there are only a few issues, b) the emotional level is moderate, c) the issues are clearly defined, d) the issues are discrete, e) there is no significant difference in power or authority between the parties, and f) the parties have the authority needed to resolve the issue or issues.

SMALL GROUP FACILITATION: If there are factions or if there is a program group or committee that is in conflict, and if one has facilitation skills, small group meetings may be a realistic option.

TEACHING/EDUCATION: Sometimes disputes arise because people lack necessary information. People may lack knowledge about the policies or doctrines of the church, for example.

COACHING: There may be a need for coaching for a period of time. Coaching has two dimensions: encouragement (reinforcing positive motivation) and demonstration of needed skills. The learners practice new skills in the presence of and with the support of someone who is well skilled and who supports the learning

MEDIATION: Mediation is appropriate normally when a conflict is between two parties or groups, although it is possible with slightly larger numbers. A qualified, experienced, and neutral person is required. Ordinarily mediation is used when the issues are clear, the parties openly acknowledge that they have a dispute, and they enter mediation voluntarily. Mediation is most commonly used as an alternative to proceeding with a formal complaint that has been or may be filed. Mediation must be protected by a provision of confidentiality, so the parties are able to make offers and provide information without fear that doing so will be used against them in case mediation fails. The outcome of mediation is usually a written agreement.

LARGE GROUP FACILITATION: Some conflicts are not merely disputes within an otherwise well-functioning healthy church. They are systemic: they affect the life and direction of the whole church. In those cases there is need to not only resolve specific issues, but to accomplish deeper and broader healing and reconciliation.

The congregation, or in large churches, a large body of people representing the various constituencies of the church, can sometimes benefit from large group facilitation. There are numerous methods, but they have in common the aim of helping the body reconsider its history, underlying values, and lifestyle as a church in preparation for planning its future. Large group facilitation of this type requires highly trained, experienced, and skillful teams of professionals.

ARBITRATION: In arbitration the parties voluntarily submit their dispute to a qualified arbitrator. The arbitrator receives input from the parties, obtains additional facts as needed, evaluates the facts and arguments, considers and protects the rights of the parties, and renders a decision. Binding arbitration allows no appeal.

DIRECTING: The church board or a higher authority may settle issues by directing action to be taken by others. Giving direction is appropriate only if the church board reaches the conclusion that those responsible at the lower level are both unable and unwilling to carry out their essential tasks.

CHAPTER 9

Conclusion

Recently I had a little practical lesson about technology. A house guest was taking pictures with his tablet and immediately sending them to various members of his family. That capacity was not new to me. But I discovered that his tablet had the ability to add filters to those pictures after they were taken. Photographers have used filters for a long time to hide or bring out certain features of their subjects. The ability for them now to add filters to pictures already taken was new, at least to me.

In this book we have filtered the information about church strife in the New Testament, in order to bring out, to highlight, the methods that were used. But let's look again at the data we have gathered using three new filters. We do this now not as thoroughly as we have done above, but to suggest areas for further investigation and dialogue.

The first filter has to do with *content*. The strife we have identified was focused on certain themes. Many of these themes are still current. One of those topics was: who is to be included in the fellowship of believers? It showed itself in the dispute over circumcision, which continued to be a point of contention throughout Paul's career, even after the Jerusalem Council (Acts 15).

For our time this question about inclusion has sometimes been about baptism (which churches acknowledge what baptisms?), about professions of faith (are doctrinal statements required by candidates for admission and how detailed?), about ordination to ministry (can women, gays, and lesbians be received on the same basis as men and heterosexuals?), and about standards of morality (is the one seeking membership in a church living according to Christian standards, as those standards are perceived by the receiving community?).

The New Testament church struggled with similar questions and was often divided over them. It is not within our scope or purpose to pronounce on or to resolve any of these issues. Instead we have hoped to shed light on the various ways early Christian communities and their leaders actually handled such conflicts. We invite the readers of this small book to look again at the above diversity of material and methods with their contemporary questions in mind.

Another area of content that caused strife was doctrine. In particular there was strife over what we call Christology. This was brightly illumined in 1–2 John, where we saw a church divided over whether Jesus Christ had actually been an enfleshed human. The Elder in these letters made the price of peace adherence to his view of Christ. Otherwise, the false teachers were liars, deceivers, and antichrists. A question for our time might be what doctrinal issues are of such importance that we are willing to be divided over them. Put more positively, what are the core Christian beliefs upon which we can find an unbreakable unity?

We are aware that for decades the ecumenical movement has been seriously at work, and with some important success, on these issues of faith and practice. Our book urges that this concern for unity be addressed creatively at the congregational level as well, and to offer some New Testament guidance for dealing with those issues.

Strife in the New Testament was sometimes about moral conduct. We have already alluded to the question of joining or remaining in a body of believers. What standards of personal conduct can and should we expect of one another? How we seek the answer to that question can be guided by studying the examples set in the early church.

Other content topics might include church leadership (and governance) and worship practices. We will leave these for others to explore.

The second filter we introduce has to do with *conflict intensity*. Put another way, it is about conflict styles. The disagreement between Paul and Barnabas in Acts 15:36–41 seems severer than the difference between Euodia and Syntyche in Philippi (Phil 4:2–3). Strife between two individuals is also less serious than the strife that affects a whole congregation, as in Corinth.

A review of the case material would show that the more severe responses, such as dicta and expulsion, occurred when the strife was both heated and widespread.

The third filter is about *perspective*. In the New Testament we see some strife responses directed toward those parties who were heatedly involved and some directed toward responsible leaders who were not party to one side of the conflict.

Leaders, such as Timothy and Titus, are advised to respond to conflicts within their purview by teaching, being examples, rebuking, being kind, correcting gently, and exhorting. Paul and other early Christian leaders expected no less of themselves. There was a set of skills that leaders needed in order to deal with strife in the early church, and early Christian communities were prepared to mobilize significant resources to respond to situations of strife.

The lesson for our time is that synods, dioceses, presbyteries, districts, and other administrative church bodies should have a set of policies to address church strife proactively and should have designated resources with appropriate skills ahead of time to deal with congregational strife.

We have attempted to answer the question of how the early Christian communities portrayed in the New Testament era responded to strife within their ranks. They responded in a whole variety of ways, which have categorized into a few major categories.

The many examples of conflict responses in the narratives of the New Testament are varied and situational. They include: dicta from various authoritative persons and to various groups and individuals, avoidance in several forms, separations of various kinds, official church actions, various kinds of teaching and mentoring, and negotiation strategies. All of this diverse material cannot be successfully reduced to a simple "mechanical" procedure, such as is often done with Matthew 18:15–17.

While conflict may be human and expected, in no case was congregational or personal conflict in the New Testament regarded as unimportant and acceptable. Conflict is so ubiquitous in the New Testament, and in churches now, that it appears to some to be a natural characteristic of the church. It is so common that it seems to be the norm, while peace in the church is the exception. A strong argument can be made that conflict in the church was and is inevitable. From that premise a conclusion is sometimes drawn that conflict should be tolerated. But, though conflict was certainly widespread, in every instance we see in the New Testament, it was never just accepted; there was always a consistent and concerted effort to move from conflict to unity.

It is also important to make a distinction between mere differences of opinion and strife in the Christian communities. This difference can be drawn by attending to the balance (or lack of balance) between the attention given to the specific issue(s) and the attention given to the relationships in individual cases. When relationships are demonstrably in danger, there is conflict, not mere differences of opinion. In many cases the language of the New Testament is focused on the failing relationships, and strong words are used to describe the situation. Some of those words are:

dissension (Gk. *stasis, dichostasia, eris*—all translated as "dissension" by the NRSV). See, e.g., Acts 15:2; Rom 16:1; 1 Cor 12:25; Gal 5:20; 1 Tim 6:4; and Titus 3:9;

dispute (Gk., *philoneikia, antilogia, maché, machomai, logomachia*—all translated as "dispute(s)" by the NRSV). See, e.g., Luke 22:24; 2 Cor 7:5; 1 Tim 6:4; and Jas 4:1–2;

quarrel(s)(ing) (Gk., *eris, diakrisis, machomai, maché*—all translated as "quarrel(s)" or "quarrelling" by the NRSV). See, e.g., Rom 13:13; 14:1; 1 Cor 1:11; 3:3; 2 Cor 12:20; Gal 5:20; 1 Tim 3:3; 2 Tim 2:23; Titus 2:2; 3:9;

division(s) (Gk., *schisma, airetikos, apodioridzo*—all translated by the NRSV as "division(s)" or "causing divisions"). See 1 Cor 10:1; 11:18; Titus 3:10; and Jude 19;

factions (Gk., *hairesis*—translated by the NRSV as "faction"). See 1 Cor 11:1; Gal 5:20; and

strife (Gk., *eris*—translated by the NRSV as "strife"). See Rom 1:29 and Gal 5:20.

Furthermore, Paul warns his readers in several places against jealousy, passing judgment on one another, offenses against each other, taking one another to court, enmities, anger, conceit, competing against each other, pride, and other similar spiritual and moral dangers. These are serious matters, and the weight of the evidence is that conflict at these levels was not to be accepted. Paul's descriptions and warnings make it clear that in every case something needed to be done to resolve the conflict.

In addition, these references show that conflict was acknowledged; it was not suppressed. Even though serious conflict was not acceptable, the Gospels, Acts, and the Epistles put it in a spotlight for all to see. Suppressing conflict would be like finding a weed in one's garden and covering it over with dirt.

Finally, the person who would serve the church by helping resolve strife must begin with his or her own personal spiritual work. We return to the quotation with which we began:

> But you, beloved, must remember the predictions of the apostles of our Lord Jesus Christ; for they said to you, "In the last time there will be scoffers, indulging their own ungodly lusts." It is these worldly people, devoid of the Spirit, who are causing divisions. But you, beloved, build yourselves up on your most holy faith; pray in the Holy Spirit; keep yourselves in the love of God; look forward to the mercy of our Lord Jesus Christ that leads to eternal

life. And have mercy on some who are wavering; save others by snatching them out of the fire; and have mercy on still others with fear, hating even the tunic defiled by their bodies (Jude 17–23).

Scripture Index